ABC–
All About Cars

Alan Trussell-Cullen

Dominie Press, Inc.

Publisher: Christine Yuen
Series Editors: Adria F. Klein & Alan Trussell-Cullen
Editors: Bob Rowland & Paige Sanderson
Illustrator: Mike Lacey
Photographer: Y. Raymond
Designers: Gary Hamada & Lois Stanfield

Published by:

🜛 **Dominie Press, Inc.**

1949 Kellogg Avenue
Carlsbad, California 92008 USA

www.dominie.com

ISBN 0-7685-0594-1

Printed in Singapore

12 V0ZF 14 13 12 11

Table of Contents

A is for *automobile*—
what this book is all about.

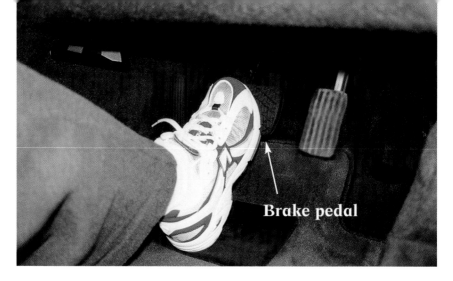

Brake pedal

B is for *brake pedal.*

C is for *car—*
another word for *automobile.*

D is for *driver.*

E is for *engine.*

7

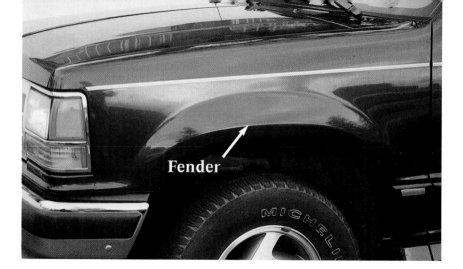

F is for *fender.*

G is for *gas.*

H is for *hood.*

I is for *Indy Car*!

Jack

J is for *jack*.

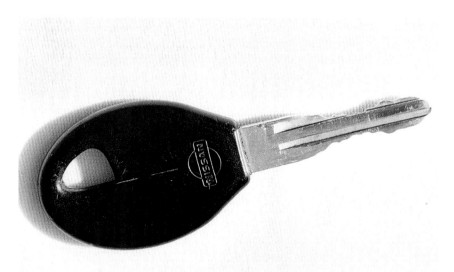

K is for *key*.

Light

L is for *light.*

M is for *mirror.*

N is for the *name* of the car.

O is for *oil*.

P is for *pedals.*

Q is for *quaint.*

Some cars *do* look quaint!

R is for *road.*

Steering
wheel

S is for *steering wheel.*

Tire ——→

T is for *tire.*

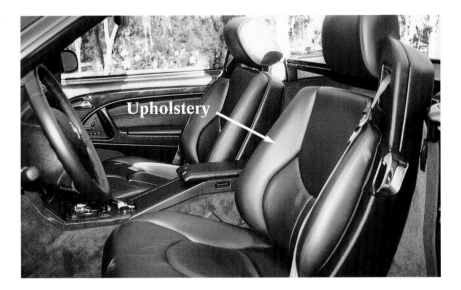

Upholstery

U is for *upholstery.*

V is for *vintage car.*

Windshield wipers

W is for *windshield wipers.*

X, Y, and **Z**?

You just might find these letters on a license plate!

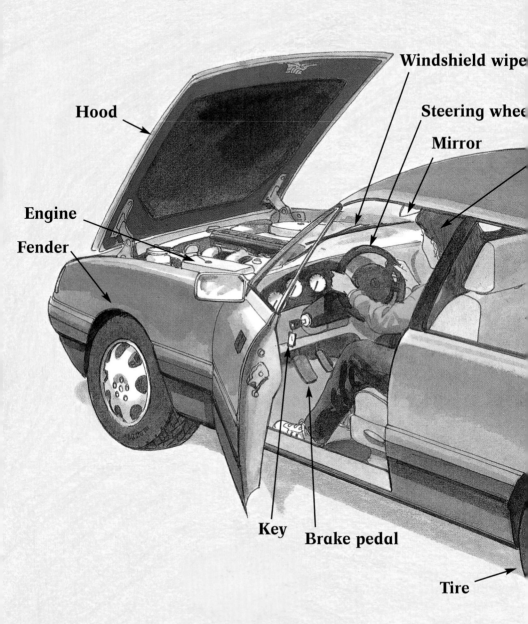

Windshield wiper

Steering wheel

Mirror

Hood

Engine

Fender

Key

Brake pedal

Tire

18

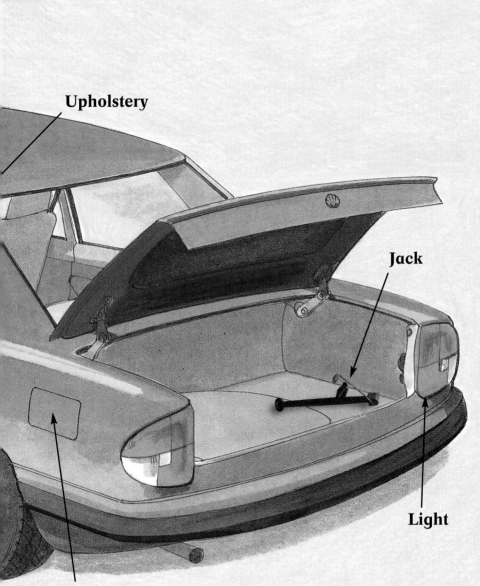

Upholstery

Jack

Light

Gas goes here

19

Picture Glossary

car:

light:

key:

mirror:

Index